BUILDING
WORLD LANDMARKS

The Berlin Wall

by Debbie Levy

BLACKBIRCH PRESS

An imprint of Thomson Gale, a part of The Thomson Corporation

THOMSON

GALE

Detroit • New York • San Francisco • San Diego • New Haven, Conn. • Waterville, Maine • London • Munich

LIBRARY OF CONGRESS CATALOGING-IN-PUBLICATION DATA

Levy, Debbie.
  The Berlin Wall / by Debbie Levy.
    p. cm. — (Building world landmarks)
Includes bibliographical references.
Summary: Discusses the Berlin Wall including why it was built, its construction, and its destruction.
  ISBN 1-4103-0137-0 (hardback : alk. paper)
  1. Berlin Wall, Berlin, Germany, 1961–1989—Juvenile literature. 2. Berlin (Germany)—History—1945–1990—Juvenile literature. 3. Germany—History—1945–1990—Juvenile literature. I. Title. II. Series.

DD881.L478 2004
943' .155087—dc22
                                                        2004006159

Table of Contents

An Invisible Wall

BEFORE A CONCRETE wall divided the city of Berlin in the summer of 1961, an invisible wall had already taken shape between the two parts of this German capital. The invisible wall separated not only East and West Berlin but also East and West Germany. It divided Eastern Europe and Western Europe. The main architects of this barrier were the Soviet Union and the United States.

The invisible wall contained no concrete, but it included other, equally formidable, components. The key ingredients were opposing ideologies, or belief systems. The Soviet Union embraced the ideology of communism. In this system, a single political party—the Communist Party—controls a nation's government and economy. The government, not individuals, owns the nation's factories, farms, shops, homes, and

Opposite:
Two women stroll along a walkway on the western side of the Berlin Wall in the mid-1980s.

Russian peasants advocate communism to their friends and neighbors in the early 1920s. Communism spread from Russia to other European countries in the twentieth century.

other property. The Communist Party makes decisions about what jobs people hold, where they live, and what education they receive.

The United States stood for a different system: representative democracy and capitalism. In a representative democracy, no single political party rules. Citizens freely elect their government representatives. Under capitalism, private individuals own property—including homes, farms, and factories—and decide for themselves where they want to live and work.

During World War II (1939–1945), the Soviet Union and the United States worked together despite

their deep ideological differences. They had a common goal: to defeat Germany, which had set out to control all of Europe. At the time, Germany was ruled by the Nazi Party and its power-hungry, hate-mongering leader, Adolf Hitler. The Soviet Union and the United States joined other nations, notably Great Britain, to fight against Nazi conquest. At a great cost in human lives, these cooperating countries—known as the Allies— defeated Nazi Germany in May 1945.

As dictator of Nazi Germany, Adolf Hitler spread terror throughout Germany and the world.

Once World War II ended, the differences between the Soviet Union and the United States became sharper than ever. The Soviet Union created Communist governments in the countries of Eastern Europe that lay along its borders. The United States and other Allies viewed the Communist expansion with fear. They were determined at least to protect Western Europe from the spread of communism.

Caught in the middle of this struggle, which became known as the Cold War, was the defeated German nation. And Berlin, the German capital, became ground zero in the fight over which ideology would prevail in Europe. In Berlin, the division between East and West took its most concrete form—a long, tall, nearly impassable wall.

The East-West Divide

IN FEBRUARY 1945, leaders of the Soviet Union, the United States, and Great Britain met to talk about the future of Germany. They agreed that at the end of the war, their nations, together with France, would occupy defeated Germany. Each of these nations, called the Four Powers, would be assigned a zone of Germany to control. Eventually, control of Germany would be returned to its citizens, who would elect a new government free of Nazi influence.

The German capital, Berlin, was located deep within the Soviet zone, in the eastern part of Germany. The Allies agreed that Berlin would also be divided into four sectors, one for each of the Four Powers. Authorities from the United States, Great Britain, and France would have free access to Berlin through the Soviet zone of Germany.

Opposite:
While Berliners watch in 1948, a man paints a boundary line on a street in Berlin, separating the British section from the Soviet section.

Stalin's Plan

On May 7, 1945, the war in Europe ended with the surrender of Germany to the Allies. The Soviet army held Berlin. This was exactly what Joseph Stalin, leader of the Soviet Union, had planned. Despite his earlier agreement to participate in Four Power rule, Stalin intended to impose communism in all of Berlin and eventually all of Germany.

For months, Stalin stalled on granting the Western powers access to Berlin. During this time, hundreds of German Communists who had waited out the war in the Soviet Union returned to Berlin. Led by a man named Walter Ulbricht, these dedicated Communists formed the core of a new, Soviet-backed government.

In July 1945, Stalin finally allowed Westerners to enter Berlin. But this did not mean the Soviets were ready to participate in Four Power rule. Instead, when the citizens of Berlin voted against a Communist city government, the Soviets forced Communist rule in the Soviet zone. They arrested and murdered Berliners in the Soviet zone who favored a democratic system.

Blockade and Airlift

Day by day, the Soviet Union intensified control of its zones in Berlin and Germany. Across Eastern Europe, the Soviets created Communist governments in Poland, Czechoslovakia, Romania, Hungary, and other countries. British statesman Winston Churchill said the Soviet Union had dropped an "iron curtain"

across Eastern Europe. It was obvious to the Western powers that the days of cooperating with the Soviets were over.

In March 1947, U.S. president Harry S. Truman announced the Truman Doctrine, a policy of resisting the spread of communism. Truman coupled this vow with a plan to provide aid to rebuild war-ravaged Europe, including Germany. Stalin rejected assistance for Eastern Europe.

With American aid, the Western sectors of Germany and Berlin were soon on the road to economic recovery. The United States, Great Britain, and France solidified democratic government in their parts of Germany and Berlin by essentially merging their three zones. Frustrated by these actions and by the Western presence in Berlin, Stalin ordered that all

German children, standing on a pile of rubble, cheer an American plane bringing food, medicine, clothing, and supplies to Berlin after the Soviet Union surrounded and closed off the city in 1948.

land routes into the city from the West be cut off, starting on June 23, 1948. Western sectors of Berlin depended on supplies from the West to survive. Through the blockade, Stalin hoped to pressure West Berliners into turning to the Communist government in East Germany for their needs.

The Western powers were as determined to preserve a democratic presence in Berlin as Stalin was determined to destroy it. If trucks and trains could not deliver supplies to West Berlin, airplanes would. For nearly eleven months, U.S. and British transport planes airlifted food, coal, medicine, and clothing to the people of West Berlin. Planes flew into the city at a rate of one every three minutes.

Two Nations, Two Berlins

Unable to push the West out of Berlin, Stalin ended the blockade on May 12, 1949. Later that month, the Western powers transformed their German zones into

With barbed wire separating them, officials of Neustadt, West Germany (foreground), talk with officials from Thuringia, East Germany.

the democratic Federal Republic of Germany, or West Germany. The independent nation adopted a constitution and held elections. Bonn became the capital of West Germany.

In October 1949, the Soviets created the German Democratic Republic, or East Germany, out of their zone. There, the German Communist Party took the helm. It restricted East Germans' ability to travel to the West. The East German government installed barbed wire and minefields along the border separating it from West Germany. The capital of East Germany was East Berlin.

In some ways, the situation in Berlin mirrored the division of the nation. The city had two separate governments—Soviet-backed Communist rule in East Berlin and democratic government in West Berlin. Unlike the nation as a whole, however, Berlin's two parts were not separated by barbed wire. In some everyday ways, the city was unified. It had a single subway system, buses and trains crossed from zone to zone, and citizens intermingled across zones.

Life in the Two Germanys

In the new West Germany, citizens enjoyed growing prosperity. West German businesses manufactured high-quality goods that were sold all over the world. With money earned from these sales, West Germans came to enjoy a high standard of living. They had plenty of food, consumer goods such as refrigerators and cars, and good homes. West Germans also enjoyed the privileges of a democratic nation, such as freedom of expression, the ability to travel, and freedom to make choices about their jobs and lives. The citizens of West Berlin shared West Germany's prosperity and freedoms.

Life in East Germany was neither prosperous nor free. Following Communist ideology, the East German government took over the nation's businesses. The Communist economic system deadened the drive of many people to work hard, since they did not personally reap the rewards of their efforts. It also led to economic hardship and shortages, since the government's central economic plans did not always result in the production of goods that people needed.

The East German government stifled not only economic activity but individual freedom. Citizens were not allowed to protest Communist ideology or government. The Communist Party controlled newspapers, radio, and television.

Subway Ride to Freedom

Many East Germans hated the Communist system. Since they were powerless to change their government through elections or protest, they chose to leave. The East German government did not permit its citizens freely to cross its border to move to the democratic West. However, East Germans were allowed to go to East Berlin. From there, they could slip into West Berlin with ease.

Beginning in 1949, thousands of East Germans left their country every year by traveling to West Berlin. American newspaper correspondents in Berlin called

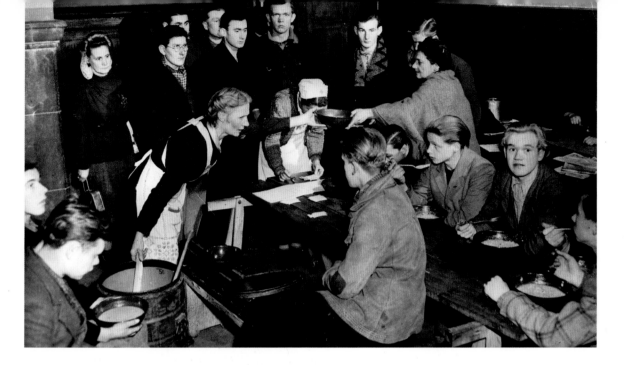

the East Germans' journey the "five-cent subway ride to freedom."[1] Once they reached West Berlin, the East Germans either stayed there or flew to West Germany.

By 1957 so many people had left that East Germany was suffering a serious shortage of workers. The government made fleeing the country a crime, but the law did not deter many East Germans. The government also tried to make the trip more difficult by diverting traffic on roads that led to West Berlin. But the East German government stopped short of closing off the two parts of the city. Such an action would have been a clear violation of the Four Power agreement that still applied to Berlin. The East German Communists and Soviets could not predict what the Western powers would do in response and did not want to risk a war.

As East Germans continued to pour out of their country, however, the Communist authorities reconsidered their options. Something had to happen.

Relief workers in West Berlin feed hot soup to some of the thousands of young refugees who began to flee from East Germany in 1949.

Chapter 2

An Overnight Sensation

By THE SUMMER of 1961, the stream of people leaving East Germany had become a flood. During the first six months of that year, 160,000 East Germans fled to West Germany. The surge of East German escapees brought to 3 million the total number who had fled since 1949. This was about equal to the population of Los Angeles at the time. It amounted to more than 15 percent of East Germany's population of 17 million.

But the numbers were not all that concerned the East German government. What was even worse, most of the fleeing East Germans were young people. Half were younger than twenty-five. More than three-quarters were under forty-five. Many were skilled and educated. They included some 16,000 engineers; 5,000 doctors, dentists, and veterinarians; 1,000 university professors and lecturers; and 15,000 high school and

Opposite:
As two young boys watch and armed East German soldiers stand guard, an East German construction crew reinforces concrete blocks on the Berlin Wall in 1961.

Walter Ulbricht reviews workers building the Berlin Wall.

elementary school teachers. East Germany was losing its workforce—and its future.

Walter Ulbricht knew that, as time passed, things would get worse. With a shrinking workforce, the nation would be able to produce fewer products, less food, and fewer homes—giving East Germans more reasons to leave.

Closely Held Secret

Ulbricht wanted to take action, but he needed the backing of his Soviet sponsors. Nikita Khrushchev, was now the leader of the Soviet Union. (Joseph Stalin had died in 1953.) In early August 1961, Ulbricht discussed the problem of the fleeing East

German population with Khrushchev. He convinced the Soviet leader to support a dramatic solution: East Germany would build a wall to keep its citizens sealed inside their own country.

For help in planning the wall, Ulbricht turned to East Germany's minister of security, Erich Honecker. Ulbricht and Honecker kept their plan a secret. They entrusted only about twenty officials with details of the plan. Others who needed to be involved were told they were preparing for some kind of police drill.

Honecker arranged for twenty-five miles (40 km) of barbed wire and thousands of concrete posts to be gathered and stored outside the city, away from prying eyes. Truck after truck delivered the posts and huge rolls of wire to police and military bases. At one East German police base, barbed wire covered a large part of the soccer field. The police who drove the trucks to the bases did not know what purpose all the wire and posts would serve.

Springing a Surprise

On Saturday, August 12, 1961, a few more East German citizens were let in on the secret plan. These were workers in the government's printing office. Once the wall went up, the government wanted to have posters ready that would inform East Berliners of the fact that the border between East Berlin and West Berlin was sealed. In the course of printing the posters, the printers naturally read them. To keep word from spreading, the printers and their families were required to stay inside their offices until midnight.

"Let Them Come to Berlin"

John F. Kennedy was president of the United States when East Germany started building the Berlin Wall. He was strongly anti-Communist but did not favor fighting the wall with military force. Instead of sending soldiers and tanks to Berlin, Kennedy went there himself. On June 26, 1963, he flew to West Berlin. He climbed an observation platform at one of the crossing points between East and West Berlin. There he saw three people waving from a building in East Berlin. He did not want to wave back, for fear of placing them in danger. But he stood quietly for a moment, recognizing their greeting.

Next, in a plaza in front of West Berlin's city hall, West Berliners crammed elbow to elbow to hear the American president give a speech (available at the John F. Kennedy Library and Museum Web site, www.cs.umb.edu/jfklibrary/). "Two thousand years ago," Kennedy began, "the proudest boast was 'civis Romanus sum' ['I am a citizen of Rome'] Today, in the world of freedom, the proudest boast is 'Ich bin ein Berliner' [I am a Berliner]."

The crowd roared its approval. "There are many people in the world who really

President John F. Kennedy was able to see the contrast between East and West Berlin as he stood on an observation platform at the Berlin Wall.

don't understand, or say they don't, what is the great issue between the free world and the Communist world," Kennedy continued. "Let them come to Berlin. There are some who say that communism is the wave of the future. Let them come to Berlin." West Berliners gave Kennedy the greatest reception of his presidency. "Ich bin ein Berliner" and "Let them come to Berlin" became celebrated around the non-Communist world.

Shortly after midnight in the early-morning hours of Sunday, August 13, 1961, the plan began to unfold. The government ordered a halt to all trains running between East Berlin and West Berlin. Soon after that, forty thousand members of the police and militia (an armed force composed mainly of factory workers) took up guard positions along the boundary between East and West Berlin. Thousands of East German soldiers stood behind them. Hundreds of Soviet and East German army tanks patrolled the outer city limits.

East German soldiers with machine guns staked out the tops of government buildings and the Brandenburg Gate, a historic monument built in 1791 and a

During the beginning stages of construction of the wall, workers strung barbed wire along a fence.

Barbed wire and armed East German policemen closed off an important crossing point between East and West Berlin at the famous Brandenburg Gate.

major crossing point between East and West Berlin. As East Berliners slept, the government issued an order forbidding the fifty-three thousand citizens who had jobs in West Berlin from holding those jobs any longer. The government further ruled that no East German could go to West Berlin without special permission.

Then, hours before daybreak on August 13, the East German government stopped all traffic between East and West Berlin. Trucks thundered into the streets of East Berlin from outlying areas carrying loads of barbed wire and concrete posts. Police set up roadblocks to keep people away from the boundary line between East and West Berlin. And on that boundary line, soldiers and laborers got to work on the project that was the cause of all the guarding and the roadblocks and the stopped trains. They started to build a wall.

A Wall of Wire

Using pneumatic drills, or jackhammers, workers tore up the streets. Then they blasted holes in the earth, cemented concrete posts into the holes, and strung barbed wire from pole to pole. Beginning at the Brandenburg Gate, they worked south toward Potsdamer Platz (Potsdam Plaza). By four in the morning, Potsdamer Platz, which had been the busiest crossing point between East and West Berlin, was closed.

By the time the 1.1 million citizens of East Berlin were getting out of bed on Sunday morning, the beginnings of a wall separated them from West Berlin. It was mostly a wall of barbed wire—really more of a fence than a wall, no more than a few feet high.

In theory, a person could cross the fence and suffer only some scratches. In reality, however, the East German guards who stood along the fence shouldering automatic weapons could inflict far more serious injuries. Some of the guards stood with their guns facing west, as if to repel efforts by West Berliners to interfere. But many guards faced east, bearing arms against their fellow citizens in East Berlin. The intent of the wall of wire was clear: to keep East Germans inside East Berlin.

Chapter 3

Concrete Curtain

As East Berliners moved about their city on Sunday, August 13, their reaction was mostly one of stunned silence. The citizens of West Berlin were far less quiet. As they watched East German laborers setting posts into the ground and stretching barbed wire across the posts, they jeered and yelled. "That's a beautiful city you have behind the barbed wire!"[2] one man shouted.

The East German workers kept on building. In some areas, they ran barbed wire down the middle of streets, separating neighbors who lived on opposite sides of the East-West border. By Monday, August 14, the wall of wire separating East and West Berlin was largely completed.

A Stronger Barrier

The cement in the fence postholes was barely dry when East Germans began escaping through the wire

Opposite:
West Germans scale the wall in 1986. As soon as the wall was built and for as long as it stood, West Berliners painted murals and graffiti on their side of the wall.

The Berlin Wall went right down the middle of some streets and suddenly West Berlin neighbors (left) were separated from their East Berlin neighbors (right).

wall to West Berlin. On August 16, an East German soldier jumped over the barbed wire into West Berlin, still dressed in his uniform. "Thank God, now I'm a free man,"[3] he said, and he threw his helmet in the air and his gun to the ground.

The East German government knew that a wire wall would not be enough to keep its citizens in East Berlin. Laborers were already at work on a stronger barrier. Using construction cranes, they lifted large concrete blocks into place and mortared them together. This concrete wall varied in height between three and six feet (0.9–1.8 m) and was topped with barbed wire.

Some streets presented unusual problems. The street and sidewalks of Harzer Strasse (Harzer Street), for example, were in West Berlin. The apartment buildings on the north side of Harzer Strasse, however, were in East Berlin. Before the wall went up, the East German residents of those apartments could simply walk across the street into West Berlin. The wall cut off this walking route to the West. From the upper floors of the apartments, however, the East German residents could see over the wall, and some saw a way out. By August 19, East German police realized that citizens were escaping into West Berlin by jumping out the windows of the four-story buildings on the north side of Harzer Strasse. To stop this, East German workers nailed shut every door of every building on that side of the street and built brick walls inside the doors and windows. The people who lived in the apartments had to move away. Their homes had become part of the Berlin Wall.

Slowly but Surely

Construction of the concrete wall proceeded hesitantly at first, as the Communists waited to see whether the Western powers would move to stop them. Some Westerners favored immediate military action to bring the East German project to a halt. But many feared that this could result in World War III—a war that could involve deadly nuclear weapons. The Western powers strongly criticized the Berlin Wall. But they did nothing to stop its construction, and the East German workers kept on building.

Work on the Berlin Wall never ended. Five years after the first barbed wire was put up, Communist soldiers were working on the wall near Potsdamer Platz in West Berlin.

By the end of August 1961, the wall of wire and concrete stretched for twenty-five miles (40 km) across Berlin. In the suburban area north of downtown, the wall consisted of barbed wire and seven-foot-high (2.1 m) concrete posts. It wound through vegetable fields and gardens. Farther south, the wall shared the landscape with factories. Closer to central Berlin, workers erected a more forbidding wall. They used concrete slabs as a base, then placed granite blocks on top of the slabs and iron bars and barbed wire atop the granite. This section of the wall, which continued into the heart of the city, was ten inches (254 mm) thick. As the wall wound out of the downtown area, it became barbed wire and concrete posts again, cutting through the southern suburbs.

In the remaining months of 1961, East German workers strengthened the wall. They added more sections of concrete slabs and blocks, along with brick walls, wooden barricades, steel stakes, and fiberboard. The wall varied in height from about five feet (1.5 m) to twelve feet (3.6 m).

Obstacle Course

The East German government did not rely on a bare wall of concrete to keep its citizens inside their country and Westerners out. As soon as the wall was up, the East Germans began to fortify it with a variety of obstacles. In November 1961, one thousand workers toiled for two days to put up special barriers of steel and concrete capable of stopping Western tanks from

Within a month after construction began, the wall of barbed wire and concrete stretched for twenty-five miles across Berlin, past churches and apartment buildings, through the downtown area into the suburbs.

Escape

Strong as the Berlin Wall was, the will of some East Germans to escape to the West was stronger. At first, people crawled through the city's sewer pipes, which carried wastewater from both parts of Berlin. Before long, East German authorities blocked the stinky underground route with metal grilles across the pipes.

With the sewers blocked, would-be escapees started digging new underground tunnels in hidden locations in East Berlin, trying to bore their way under the wall. In one case, NBC, the American television network, provided money to a tunnel-digging group in exchange for the right to film the project. NBC created a television special about the tunnel, broadcast in December 1962. It attracted a greater audience than the popular *I Love Lucy* show that aired at the same time on another network.

Tunneling was difficult and expensive, so people devised other escape methods. Some swam across waterways to reach West Berlin, evading East German patrol boats. One young couple swam across the Havel River in September 1961, pushing their eighteen-month-old baby along in a rubber tub. Others flew over the wall in hot-air balloons, until the East German government outlawed the sale

East Berliners dug secret tunnels like this one to try to escape the Communist government.

of lightweight cloth that could be used to build such aircraft. Citizens who managed to reach the wall on foot used rope to climb over to the West. It did not take long for the Communist authorities to ban the sale of rope.

It is not known for certain how many people tried to get across the wall. According to one reliable estimate, 10,000 people tried to escape over the years the wall stood, but only 5,000 succeeded. At least 239 people died during their escape attempts, many from gunshot wounds inflicted by East German border guards.

crashing the wall in downtown Berlin. To prevent vehicles in East Berlin from approaching the wall, workers dug ditches deep enough to trap cars and trucks that attempted to cross them.

One of the most formidable obstacles created on the East Berlin side of the wall was a wide area known as the "forbidden zone." The forbidden zone, also known as the "death strip," was planted with mines to discourage anyone from entering it. A road ran parallel to the forbidden zone, allowing East German guards to drive along the wall to inspect and patrol it. Next to the road, the East Germans laid out a strip of sand and gravel, raked smooth so guards could see the footprints of anyone trying to escape.

Construction workers in East Germany were kept busy building another key component of the wall's fortifications —a series of watchtowers. Eventually, the East Germans built nearly three hundred watchtowers, each about thirty feet (3 m) tall and ten feet (9.1 m) square. High in the towers, guards looked down on the forbidden zone and the nearby wall. They were under orders to shoot to kill any East Germans who tried to cross.

This watchtower near the Brandenburg Gate was one of three hundred towers the Communists built to guard the wall and the forbidden zone.

The East German government went to still greater lengths to prevent its citizens from approaching or crossing the wall. Dogs on sixty-foot (18 m) leashes patrolled the forbidden zone. In some areas, soldiers rigged guns to fire automatically when a person crossed a trip wire near the wall.

Encircling the City

So far, East Germany's leaders had sealed East Berlin from West Berlin. But Berlin was completely surrounded by East Germany, like an island in the sea.

West Berlin's north, south, and west borders touched on areas of East Germany that were not blocked off by any wall. The government was concerned that its citizens might still slip into West Berlin over those borders.

So the wall builders kept building. When construction workers were finished dividing Berlin, they extended the wall to run along the line that separated West Berlin from the East Germany territory that surrounded it. In the end, the Berlin Wall was more than one hundred miles (160 km) long. If straightened, it could have reached from New York City to Philadelphia.

Sharp pieces of metal were placed at the top of the wall to discourage people from attempting to climb over the wall.

An Unending Job

Work on the wall was never completely finished. Weather and pollution caused some parts to crumble. The wall and its fortifications required ongoing construction to keep the barrier from falling into disrepair.

East German authorities were always looking for ways to make the wall stronger. They accomplished this by upgrading the concrete elements of the wall. In the mid-1970s, the East Germans developed a new type of concrete segment, which they used to repair and replace extensive portions of the wall. Each new segment weighed more than six thousand pounds (2751 kg) and was nearly twelve feet (3.6 m) high, four feet (1.2 m) wide, and six inches (152 mm) thick. With steel mesh sandwiched inside, the new segments were more resistant to breakthroughs by cars and trucks than the older concrete slabs had been.

On top of every new concrete segment, workers installed another innovation: a pipe forty centimeters (nearly sixteen inches) in diameter. A pipe of this size is very difficult for a person to grasp. It presented a final barrier to anyone who might approach and climb the twelve-foot (3.6 m) wall. If a person reached the top, the pipe ensured that he or she would find it almost impossible to hang on long enough to vault to the other side. The East German leaders seemed to have reached their goal of building a wall that their citizens could not get over, under, through, or around.

Chapter 4

It All Falls Down

THE BERLIN WALL transformed the city of Berlin. Residents of the city, East and West, were never far from a landscape of concrete panels. The wall cut through 192 streets. It intersected thirty-two railway lines, eight suburban train lines, four subway lines, three superhighways (called autobahns), and several rivers and lakes. (In the waterways, the wall consisted of underwater fencing.) East German authorities left several heavily barricaded openings in the wall as crossing points for selected West Germans and foreigners. However, authorities strictly regulated and limited the comings and goings of such individuals.

Standing Strong

From time to time, the East German government eased restrictions on who could pass through the wall's crossing points. Early in the life of the wall, for

Opposite:
East German citizens climb the wall at the Brandenburg Gate after the East German border was opened on November 10, 1989.

West Germans enjoy a picnic by the wall in this photograph from 1981.

example, East Germany agreed that West Berliners could visit East Berlin during the Christmas and New Year's holiday season. Few East Germans, however, were allowed to visit the West.

In West Berlin, tourists flocked to certain segments of the wall to climb observation posts and peer over into East Berlin. East Berliners could not similarly catch a glimpse of West Berlin, but they were aware of the differences between the two halves of the city. Radio broadcasts and visitors from the West painted a vivid picture of the prosperity and freedom on the other side of the wall.

Meanwhile, in the Soviet Union, major changes were under way. In March 1985, Mikhail Gorbachev became leader of that country. Recognizing that his country was not prospering under communism, Gorbachev began to revise his nation's economic system and government. He embraced two policies that became famous around the world: glasnost (openness) and perestroika (restructuring, or democratic reform). The Soviet Union was on its way to a new era.

Cracks in the Barrier

Gorbachev encouraged the heads of other Communist countries to follow his lead. In 1989, Communist Hungary and Czechoslovakia increased freedoms for their citizens. Hungary also opened its border with Austria, which was a representative democracy. East Germany, however, remained in the grip of old-style communism. Erich Honecker, now East Germany's leader, said of the wall in January 1989: "It will still stand in fifty or one hundred years."[4]

But because of changes in Hungary and Czechoslovakia, East Germans were no longer completely cut off from the West. East Germans had always been allowed to visit those two Communist countries. Now, with Hungary letting people cross the border into Austria, many East Germans took advantage of this opening to the West. They simply traveled to Hungary as if going on vacation. From there, they slipped over into Austria and then to West Germany. Similarly,

Mikhail Gorbachev encouraged Communist countries to revise their economic systems because he realized that communism was not working.

East Germans in Czechoslovakia went to the West German embassy there, which helped them make their way West.

As was the case twenty-eight years earlier, thousands of East Germans were once again leaving their country. The East German government had built a one-hundred-mile (160 km) wall to keep its citizens from leaving. Now it could impose further restrictions on travel by East Germans—or it could embrace Gorbachev's new openness.

The Wall Falls

With East Germany at this crossroads, Gorbachev visited East Berlin in October 1989. In his speeches he addressed the need for change. After Gorbachev's visit, East Germany erupted in protests against the Honecker regime. In cities across East Germany, millions marched to demand freedom to travel, freedom of speech, and free elections.

In the past, the East German government had violently put down protests. But these new demonstrations were so massive that the government would have had to wage war against its own people to suppress them. Within the ruling Communist Party, some leaders saw that change was unavoidable. On October 18, they forced Honecker out of office. A different Communist official became the new East German leader.

But East German citizens wanted more than just a new face on their nation's leadership, and the protests continued. In the midst of the upheaval, a Communist Party official held a press conference on the

evening of November 9, 1989. The official, Gunter Schabowski, discussed the ongoing crisis and announced a new government policy. East Germans, he said, would be permitted to travel directly to the West. He did not provide details. Then a reporter asked Schabowski when the new travel policy would take effect. Schabowski seemed unprepared for the question. But after fumbling for a few moments, he responded, "Right away."[5]

The news spread like wildfire. In Berlin, people flocked to the wall, and without violence, border guards let them approach it. They watched as young people hoisted themselves on top of the concrete segments. At midnight, the guards opened barricades at the wall's crossing points and waved through anybody who wanted to cross.

Thousands of people gathered at the Berlin Wall in November 1989 when it was announced that, under a new travel policy, East Germans would be permitted to travel directly to the West.

Thousands of East Berliners ventured into the Western half of the city in the early hours of November 10. They strolled about the streets, shops, and cafés of West Berlin. At three in the morning, the streets were filled with people. West Berliners too flocked to the border to join the celebration. One taxi driver, who had left East Berlin in 1960, was thrilled to find his taxi surrounded by people. "A traffic jam!" he exclaimed. "It's a perfect, beautiful traffic jam!"[6]

Taking It Down

As the day wore on, hundreds of thousands of East Berliners traveled to West Berlin. Many had joyful reunions with family and friends. At the end of

On November 10, 1989, thousands of West Berliners rallied in front of the Brandenburg Gate to celebrate the new freedom given to their East German neighbors.

the historic day, November 10, 1989, nearly all the East Berliners—after years of yearning for the chance to cross into West Berlin—went home to East Berlin. With the freedom to travel, the people no longer felt compelled to run away.

In the days that followed, East German guards created more openings in the wall. Workers operated bulldozers to push sections aside. Some people, called "woodpeckers," chipped away at the wall, taking pieces as souvenirs.

One hundred miles of wall did not fall in a day, or even a week. The wall still stood, but it was riddled with holes. Similarly, the Communist East German government was breaking apart. Leadership in the Communist Party changed. The new leaders announced that they would allow free elections in East Germany.

Four months after the wall began coming down, in March 1990, East Germans voted in their first free elections in more than fifty years. They elected officials dedicated to throwing off communism and reunifying with West Germany. Reunification became effective on October 3, 1990. The remaining soldiers of the Four Powers that had occupied Berlin after World War II left the city. Finally, Berlin was no longer an occupied zone. In 1999, it became the capital of unified Germany.

After the border was opened, workers with bulldozers created more openings in the wall, and ordinary citizens used hammers to chip away souvenir pieces.

A Concrete Canvas

To some people, a blank wall is an invitation to scribble—that is, to create graffiti. From the pyramids of ancient Egypt to the New York City subways, structures around the world have served as backdrops for graffiti artists. The Berlin Wall was one more very large concrete canvas.

East Germans were kept away from their side of the wall by armed guards, so only the West side of the wall became a giant

The West German side of the wall became a giant canvas for art, anti-Communist protests, and personal scribbling.

mural. Using spray paint, both famous artists and unknown scribblers drew on the wall. Many created large pictures. Others wrote messages. Much of the art expressed an anti-Communist viewpoint. Some was simply personal.

The East German government had carefully placed the wall entirely within its territory, away from the actual border with the West. The government wanted its soldiers to be able to go around to the West Berlin side, while

remaining on East Berlin territory, to make inspections and repairs. Technically, therefore, the Western graffiti artists were in East German territory when they drew on the wall. However, East German guards did not patrol the West Berlin side of the wall, and the artists were undisturbed. From time to time, East German workers painted over the graffiti with white paint—and the blank wall would fill up with fresh images.

An American tourist shakes hands with an East German border guard through a hole in the Berlin Wall just a couple of weeks after the barricades were taken down.

Remnants of the Wall

As the two Germanys and two Berlins transformed themselves, the wall began to disappear. By November 1991, government workers had destroyed most of it. They left only small sections to serve as memorials to those who died trying to escape and as historic landmarks. Concrete blocks from the wall were turned into road-building material. Other segments of the wall were put on display around the world.

Today, the wall barely has a footprint in Berlin. A row of cobblestones winds twelve miles (19.3 km) through downtown Berlin, marking where the wall once stood. The concrete and barbed wire are mostly gone, but the wall's impact on the minds of the people of Germany and Berlin is unlikely to be erased for a long, long time.

Notes

Chapter One: The East-West Divide

1. Norman Gelb, *The Berlin Wall*. New York: Times Books, 1986, p. 5.

Chapter Three: Concrete Curtain

2. Harry Gilroy, "Berliners of Both Sides Tense," *New York Times,* August 15, 1961, p. 8.
3. Quoted in *New York Times*, "East German Soldier Defects with Well-Timed Jump," August 17, 1961, p. 10.

Chapter Four: It All Falls Down

4. Quoted in Peter Wyden, *Wall: The Inside Story of Divided Berlin*. New York: Simon and Schuster, 1989, p. 681.
5. Quoted in Andrea Schulte-Peevers, *Berlin*, 3rd ed. London: Lonely Planet, 2002, p. 20.
6. Quoted in Gerhard Rempel, "The Wall Cracks: November 9, 1989," Berlin 2000 Lectures, Western New England College, http://mars.vnet.wnec.edu/~grempel/courses/berlin/lectures/lectures.html.

Chronology

1945   Nazi Germany surrenders to the Allies in May, ending World War II in Europe. The country and city of Berlin are each divided into four temporary zones. Each zone is occupied by one of the Four Powers—the United States, Great Britain, France, and the Soviet Union.

1948   The Soviet Union begins its blockade of Berlin in June, refusing to allow overland traffic and supplies from the West to enter the city. In response, the Western Allies begin the Berlin airlift to bring supplies to the people of Berlin by plane.

1949   The Soviet Union lifts the Berlin blockade in May. The Federal Republic of Germany (West Germany) and the German Democratic Republic (East Germany) are formed.

1957   The East German government prohibits its citizens from leaving the country without permission.

1961   The East German government begins to build the Berlin Wall on August 13.

1963   U.S. president John F. Kennedy visits West Berlin in June and makes a famous speech in which he says, "Ich bin ein Berliner," or "I am a Berliner."

1989   In November, the government of East Germany opens the border between East and West Germany and creates openings in the Berlin Wall.

1990   East German workers begin to take down the Berlin Wall. East and West Germany unite into a single united German nation.

1991   The last segments of the Berlin Wall come down.

1999   Berlin becomes the capital of Germany again.

Glossary

allies—Nations that cooperate with each other, often against a common enemy in war.

barbed wire—Wire made of twisted strands formed into sharp barbs, or points.

blockade—The forced isolation of an area by cutting off transportation routes into and out of it.

capitalism—An economic system in which individuals and private companies own property, including land, factories, farms, and shops.

communism—A system of government in which a single political party is in control, and the party and government also control the economy.

democracy—A system of government in which people rule themselves, almost always by some form of majority rule.

ideology—A system of beliefs, often about a nation's system of government and economy.

mine—A deadly device, often buried or hidden in the ground, that explodes when a person or vehicle comes in contact with it.

Nazi Germany—The rule of Germany from 1933 to 1945 under Adolf Hitler and his Nazi Party.

For More Information

Books

Craig Blohm, *The Cold War: An Uneasy Peace.* San Diego: Lucent Books, 2002.

Britta Bjornlund, *The Cold War Ends.* San Diego: Lucent Books, 2003.

Doris Epler, *Berlin Wall: How It Rose and Why It Fell.* Brookfield, CT: Millbrook, 1992.

Scott Ingram, *Joseph Stalin.* San Diego: Blackbirch Press, 2002.

Jeffrey B. Symynkywicz, *Germany: United Again.* Parsippany, NJ: Dillon, 1996.

Web Sites

The Berlin Wall, Ten Years After (www.time.com). *Time* magazine's look back at the Berlin Wall ten years after it came down includes magazine articles, a photo essay, and brief biographies of the main people involved.

A Concrete Curtain: The Life and Death of the Berlin Wall (www.wall-berlin.org). Compelling information and photographs, organized by a French-German museum partnership.

The Lost Border: Photographs of the Iron Curtain (www.brianrose.com). Excellent photographs showing the Berlin Wall in its last years, beginning in 1987.

The Rise and Fall of the Berlin Wall (www.newseum.org). Easy-to-follow summary of events, with a special focus on the role of the news media, presented by a Washington, D.C., museum of the media.

Index
and About the Author

Index

About the Author

Before she started writing books for children, Debbie Levy earned a bachelor's degree in government and foreign affairs from the University of Virginia, as well as a law degree and master's degree in world politics from the University of Michigan. She practiced law with a large Washington, D.C., law firm and worked as a newspaper editor. Her previous books for children include books for Blackbirch's sister presses, KidHaven Press and Lucent Books, about slave life, Maryland, civil liberties, bigotry, and medical ethics. Debbie enjoys paddling around in kayaks and canoes and fishing in the Chesapeake Bay region. She lives with her husband, two sons, a dog, and a cat in Maryland.